❖ GREAT LITTLE COOK BOOKS ❖

Wholefood

COOKING

Healthy eating to enjoy

It is easy to begin eating a wholefood diet with
fresh natural foods, prepared with care. Take small
steps at first. The following pages will tell you what
to do. You will soon discover how good wholefood
tastes and how well you feel on a wholefood diet.
Sensible wholefood eating provides all the
nutritional and active agents necessary to keep
both body and spirit in top condition. You will
find the ingredients and spices that may be
unfamiliar to you in health-food or wholefood
shops, who will be happy to advise you.

Colour photography by
Odette Teubner and Kerstin Mosny.

AURA

CONTENTS

THE WHOLEFOOD DIET

The wholefood diet is founded upon plant foods, such as wholegrains, vegetables, fruit and pulses. These are complemented with milk and dairy products, while meat, fish and eggs play only a subordinate part. Highly processed foods, such as refined flour, white sugar, refined oils and food additives, have no place in a wholefood diet. 'Let our food be as natural as possible,' was the guiding principle coined by the doctor and food scientist Professor Werner Kollath about 50 years ago. This means that a wholefood diet should consist of fresh, seasonal and, preferably, organically grown produce. Food should be prepared as carefully as possible, using little fat. About half our daily intake should comprise raw fresh foods because they still contain all the essential nutrients, some of which can be destroyed by cooking. Besides vegetables, fruit and herbs, these include cereals, nuts, seeds, milk and dairy products made without heating, and cold-pressed vegetable oils.

The five basics of the wholefood diet

1. Wholegrain cereals: Wheat, rye, oats, barley, millet, maize, rice, buckwheat, spelt and green spelt grain should be served as often as possible. Spelt is an ancient kind of grain, related to wheat, and green spelt grain is simply early harvested spelt. It is popular in northern Europe and is available from some wholefood shops. It is possible to buy special strains of oats and barley which grow without husks and are still capable of germinating. Buckwheat is not a cereal, but a kind of knot-grass and can be used exactly like a cereal.

Wholegrains contain nearly all nutrients necessary to life, including vitamins, minerals, fats, high-quality proteins and secondary proteins. Highly refined white flour, on the other hand, is an 'empty' carbohydrate, lacking nearly all these elements. The indigestible fibre in wholegrains has an important function. It makes you feel full more quickly and for longer, stimulates the digestive processes and activates the bowels. It helps to lower cholesterol levels and to regulate blood sugar levels.

2. Vegetables and fruit: These are not only rich in vitamins and minerals, but also provide aroma, colour, flavour and natural antibiotics. Their health-giving properties have been known and used in natural medicine for centuries. Modern research has shown that many vegetables contain vital antioxidants which play a major role in the prevention of a wide range of diseases, including many cancers.

3. Pulses: Nutritionally, peas, beans, lentils and other pulses perfectly complement vegetables. They provide protein, many B group vitamins and minerals, especially iron, and fibre.

4. Natural fats and oils: These are important in the diet, but should be consumed only in moderation (maximum 70–80 g/$2^1/_2$–$3^1/_4$ oz per day). Cold-pressed, unrefined oils are the most valuable. They contain a high proportion of polyunsaturated fatty acids – including the vital linoleic acid – and vitamins.

They can be used as follows:
• for salads – all seed oils, sunflower oil and olive oil
• for braising – sunflower, olive, grapeseed, soya and corn oils, butter and soft vegetable margarine
• as a spread – butter and soft vegetable margarine
• for frying – sunflower, olive, grapeseed, soya and corn oils
• for baking – all the fats named above are suitable. Refined oils and hydrogenated (hard) margarine are less valuable.

5. Milk and dairy products: These are important sources of calcium and vitamins A and B, but are high in fats. Raw, untreated, unpasteurized milk is best, but it is essential that it comes from a properly tested and certified herd. It should be avoided by the very young, very old, the infirm, those with an impaired immune system and pregnant women. UHT (ultra-heat treatment), also known as long-life milk,

4

sterilized milk and condensed milk have all undergone nutritional damage through heating. They have no place in the wholefood diet. Souring and maturing makes milk more digestible. This is especially true of various kinds of soured dairy products, such as crème fraîche, yogurt, smetana, curd, cottage and cream cheese, as well as un-pasteurized cheese.

Meat, fish and eggs are not necessary for a healthy, balanced diet. They are a useful source of high-quality proteins, but may also contain a high level of saturated fats that can raise cholesterol levels in the blood. However, eating them occasionally will not necessarily do any harm. 'Occasionally' means one or two servings of meat and fish and one or two eggs per

From top left above to bottom right: millet, buckwheat, wheat, barley, maize, spelt, oats, rye and green spelt grain

week. Sticking to this is not really very difficult and you will soon find that your taste for meat decreases when you eat a wholefood diet. Even if you give up meat, fish and eggs entirely, you need not worry about lack of protein, because vegetarian foods can be combined to provide a protein mixture as – or even more – nutritious as animal protein. Combining vegetable proteins with a small quantity of animal proteins is also a very healthy way to eat. Optimal combinations (for one meal) are:

• wholegrain + pulses
• wholegrain + nuts
• wholegrain or potatoes + milk or dairy products (for example yogurt, curd cheese, hard cheese)
• potatoes + egg.

Complicated nutritional calculations are not necessary. The more varied your daily menus, the better you combine the nutrients of different foods. In fact, it would be true to say that variety is the keystone of a healthy and balanced diet.

Natural sweeteners

Clearly, refined sugar is not used in wholefood cooking, as it provides only 'empty' calories, which make you fat, and it removes vitamins from the body. However, you should also be sparing with natural sweeteners, such as honey, apple and pear juice, syrup, treacle, brown sugar and dried fruits. They also contain between 60 and `

93 per cent sugar and, if used excessively, can damage your health as much as refined sugar. The best and most natural way to sweeten dishes is with sweet, ripe fruit, such as pears, plums, bananas, fresh dates and figs.

Drinks

Quench your thirst with mineral water, good tap water, unsweetened herb and fruit teas, cereal-based 'coffee' and diluted fruit and vegetable juices. Make sure that the sodium content of mineral water is below 170 mg per litre (sodium-reduced) and do not always drink the same brand, as the mineral content varies between them.

Coffee, tea, beer and wine are stimulants and should be

drunk only very occasionally and in small quantities. Soft drinks, packed with sugar or artificial sweeteners, have no place in the wholefood diet. They cause a rapid release of sugar into the bloodstream, providing an instant 'lift', but this is quickly followed by a surge of insulin, which pulls the blood sugar level down again, with a resultant sudden drop in energy.

Drink about five glasses of water each day. Do not wait until you are thirsty – your body is already dehydrated.

Do-it-yourself wholegrains

Cereal grain which is capable of sprouting is a long-lasting 'natural preserver'. As soon as the grain is broken or crushed, many of its nutrients are attacked by the oxygen in the air. It loses its aroma and may become bitter. Freshly ground or freshly crushed grain is best and it should be used as soon as possible. Some wholefood and health-food shops will grind small quantities of wholegrains specially. Store it in a tightly closed container in a cool, dry and dark place. It will keep for about four weeks in the refrigerator or the freezer.

Wholegrains remain capable of sprouting for one to two years if stored in a cool, dry and airy place, such as in linen or paper sacks or boxes made of untreated wood. Every

All sorts of natural sweeteners can be used instead of refined sugar, such as fresh fruits, syrup or brown sugar.

time you use some of the grain, stir the remainder to improve the air circulation and deter pests. Real enthusiasts can obtain their own small mill to grind it themselves.

Germinating seeds

Compared with other salad vegetables, sprouting seeds provide significant quantities of minerals, particularly potassium, calcium, phosphorus, magnesium and iron. During sprouting, the vitamin and protein content increases, while the fat content decreases and carbohydrates are broken down or converted. Pulses become more digestible.

All you require to grow your own sprouts are the seeds, water, warmth, light and air. They should be in a light place, but not in direct sunlight and at an even temperature of about 15–20°C/59–68°F.

You do not need a special sprouter, although these are convenient and inexpensive. You can germinate seeds in a sieve (only suitable for large seeds) or in a jam jar. Wash the seeds in a bowl of cold water and leave them to soak for 12 hours or overnight. Drain off the water through a sieve and rinse well. Put the sieve over a bowl and cover two-thirds of it with a glass plate so that the air can still circulate. Rinse the seeds morning and evening with cold water, until the seedlings are about 3 mm/1/8 inch long. Alternatively, pour the soaked

seeds into a 1.5 litre/2 1/2 pint glass container and cover the top with muslin held in place with an elastic band. Rinse the seeds twice a day and drain them thoroughly.

To grow seeds in a sprouter, rinse them well in cold water and place them in the bottom two layers of the sprouter. Replace the lid and put the sprouter in a light place, out of direct sunlight, and at an even temperature of about 15–20°C/59–68°F. Water the seeds with fresh cold water twice a day, remembering to tip away the excess that gathers in the base of the sprouter (otherwise the sprouts will rot).

Freshly harvested sprouts can be used immediately or stored in the salad drawer of the refrigerator for up to a week.

Whichever method you choose, always use beans or seeds that are intended for cooking or sprouting, rather than those intended for planting outdoors in the garden, as the latter have often been treated with preservatives or other horticultural chemicals.

The following beans, peas and seeds are simple to sprout, widely available and provide a highly nutritious and flavoursome addition to salads, stir-fries and many other dishes.

aduki beans
alfalfa
black poppy seeds
chick-peas
fenugreek seeds
lentils
linseed
mung beans
pumpkin seeds
sesame seeds
soya beans
sunflower seeds
wheat
white poppy seeds

A word about rice

A staple for a large part of the world's population, rice is both nutritious and tasty. Brown rice is the wholegrain with only the outer husk removed. The layers of bran are retained and it is these which give brown rice its characteristic colour, chewy texture and nutty flavour. It contains more protein than white rice and is richer in minerals and vitamins, including calcium, iron and several B group vitamins. Available in long, medium and short grain, it can be substituted for white rice in any recipe, but takes longer to cook – up to 45 minutes – although cooking time can be

Cereal grains should always be stored in a cool, airy and dry place. You can buy special storage sacks.

Cooking wholegrains

Per 100 g/3³/4 oz wholegrains	Liquid	Soaking time (hours)	Cooking time (minutes)	Standing time (minutes)
Wheat Rye Barley	200 ml/7 fl oz	6–12	40–60	20–30
Spelt	200 ml/7 fl oz	6–12	10	15
Green spelt grain	150 ml/¹/4 pint	none	20	20
Oats	150 ml/¹/4 pint	none	40–45	10–15
Whole rice	200 ml/7 fl oz	6–12	20	10–15
Millet	200–250 ml/ 7–8 fl oz	none	5	15–20
Buckwheat	200 ml/7 fl oz	none	2–5	10–15

reduced by soaking the rice first. It will absorb about four times its own volume of liquid. Enriched rice is white rice with some of the nutrients, notably iron and some of the B group vitamins, put back after the grains have been polished during refining.

Baking with wholegrains
You can make sweet and spicy dishes from any kind of cereal, but only wheat, spelt and rye are suitable for baking because they contain gluten. As whole-meal flour absorbs more liquid than white flour, wholemeal dough is always wetter than dough made from white flour. Wholemeal flour also absorbs liquid during baking.

Boiling wholegrains
1. Pick over the grains, if necessary, to remove any dirt. Rinse the grains in a sieve under cold running water and drain. Soak them for several hours in cold water or un-salted vegetable stock. This 'unlocks' the grains so that the minerals they contain are more readily available to the body. (Crushed or ground grain requires only about 30–60 minutes soaking time.) Soaking also reduces the cooking time, saving energy and cost and preserving heat-sensitive vitamins.
2. Boil the grains in their soaking liquid in a saucepan with a well-fitting lid. Only then add salt or vegetable

stock granules, otherwise the cooking time is lengthened and the grains (especially wheat, rye and oats) do not become tender. Then leave to stand on the turned-off hob.
3. Millet and buckwheat are exceptions. They are washed when they are hot and put into boiling liquid, so that they remain grainy.
4. Stir crushed or ground grain with a whisk in cold or warm liquid. Boil it, stirring constantly, for 2–10 minutes, depending on how finely ground it is, and then leave to stand for about 10 minutes on the turned-off hob.

Milk and dairy products provide important vitamins and minerals.

Savoy cabbage with fennel and tomatoes

Quick

Serves 2
15 ml/1 tablespoon cider vinegar
15 ml/1 tablespoon white
    wine vinegar
1.5 ml/1/4 teaspoon herb salt
45 ml/3 tablespoons sunflower oil
1 small onion, very finely chopped
150 g/5 oz Savoy
    cabbage, shredded
150 g/5 oz fennel
2 ripe tomatoes, diced
15 ml/1 tablespoon chopped
    fresh parsley

Approximately per portion:
1,100 kj/260 kcal
6 g protein
18 g fat
12 g carbohydrate
7 g fibre

● Approximate preparation
  time: 20 minutes

1. Combine the cider vinegar, white wine vinegar and salt. Beat in the oil, a tablespoon at a time, then stir in the chopped onion. Set the dressing aside.

2. Place the cabbage on serving plates. Cut the fennel into quarters and then into thin strips. Arrange the fennel on top of the cabbage to leave a green border around it.

3. Top with the tomatoes, placing them in the middle of the salads. Sprinkle the salads with the vinaigrette dressing and scatter the parsley over them.

Tip

Herb salt consists of about 15 per cent dried herbs and 85 per cent cooking or sea salt. It both seasons and flavours the dish. It is even better if you can use fresh herbs and then season sparingly with plain sea salt. (Too much salt can be harmful.)

Celeriac salad with carrots and courgettes

Easy

Serves 2
75 ml/5 tablespoons
    single cream
75 ml/5 tablespoons
    natural yogurt
5 ml/1 teaspoon Dijon mustard
30 ml/2 tablespoons lemon juice
150 g/5 oz celeriac
150 g/5 oz young courgettes
115 g/4 oz carrots
30 ml/2 tablespoons chopped fresh
    mixed herbs, such as parsley,
    chives, lemon balm
    and tarragon
sea salt
45 ml/3 tablespoons pumpkin
    seeds, to garnish

Approximately per portion:
1,200 kj/285 kcal
11 g protein
21 g fat
11 g carbohydrate
7 g fibre

● Approximate preparation
  time: 30 minutes

1. Beat together the cream, yogurt, mustard, lemon juice and a pinch of salt in a large bowl to form a creamy dressing.

2. Reserve any leaves from the celeriac. Peel the root and grate it into the dressing. Finely chop the reserved leaves and add them to the dressing.

3. Grate the courgettes and carrots or cut them into fine matchsticks and add to the salad.

4. Add the chopped mixed herbs to the salad and toss gently together. Scatter the pumpkin seeds on top.

Variation
You can use finely chopped chicory instead of celeriac and replace the pumpkin seeds with chopped hazelnuts.

Tip

Celeriac is a knobbly and rather unattractive root vegetable, which may account for its lack of popularity. However, it has a deliciously nutty flavour, rather sweeter than celery. It is not often sold with its top intact.

*Above: Savoy cabbage with fennel and tomatoes
Below: Celeriac salad with carrots and courgettes*

Fennel and apple salad with orange dressing

Economical • Easy

Serves 2
75 ml/5 tablespoons
    whipping cream
115 ml/7 tablespoons
    natural yogurt
5 ml/1 teaspoon Dijon mustard
juice of ¹/2 orange
juice of ¹/2 lemon
250 g/9 oz fennel
1 large red eating apple
sea salt
6 walnuts, halved, to garnish

Approximately per portion:
1,500 kj/360 kcal
8 g protein
24 g fat
26 g carbohydrate
8 g fibre

● Approximate preparation
  time: 20 minutes

---

1. To make the dressing, beat the cream in a small bowl until thickened and fairly stiff. Stir in the yogurt, mustard, orange and lemon juice and season to taste with salt. Cover with clear film and set aside in the refrigerator until required.

2. Cut off and reserve the feathery fennel fronds for the garnish. Cut the fennel bulb in half lengthways, then thinly slice it across.

3. Quarter and core the apple, then cut it into thin slices.

4. Place the fennel and apple in a serving bowl, add the dressing and toss gently to coat. Garnish the salad with the walnut halves and the reserved fennel fronds and serve immediately.

Tip

The salad is best served immediately. If you need to prepare it in advance, as soon as you have prepared the salad ingredients, mix them with the dressing or with a vinaigrette, then cover the bowl with clear film. This helps to preserve vitamins that are sensitive to light and oxygen.

Pear and pumpkin salad with cheese dressing

Exquisite

Serves 2
115 g/4 oz soft blue-veined cheese,
    such as dolcelatte
120 ml/4 fl oz buttermilk
15–30 ml/1–2 tablespoons
    chopped fresh mixed herbs,
    such as parsley, tarragon and
    lemon balm
¹/4 head endive
1 ripe pear
150 g/5 oz celeriac
150 g/5 oz pumpkin
10 ml/2 teaspoons lemon juice
2 ripe, firm tomatoes, sliced
10 ml/2 teaspoons snipped
    fresh chives
15 ml/1 tablespoon finely
    chopped walnuts

Approximately per portion:
1,600 kj/380 kcal
19 g protein
22 g fat
24 g carbohydrate
10 g fibre

● Approximate preparation
  time: 25 minutes

---

1. Purée the cheese with a hand-held mixer or mash it well with a fork. Add the buttermilk and beat thoroughly to a smooth dressing. Stir in the herbs.

2. Cut the endive into thin strips and arrange it on a serving plate. Quarter and core the pear and cut it into thin slices. Peel the celeriac and cut it into thin matchsticks. Cut the pumpkin flesh into matchsticks and sprinkle with the lemon juice.

3. Arrange all the salad ingredients decoratively on top of the bed of endive. Sprinkle the tomatoes with the chives and the pumpkin with the walnuts. Serve immediately with the dressing.

Above: Fennel and apple salad with orange dressing
Below: Pear and pumpkin salad with cheese dressing

Avocado salad with celery

Exquisite

Serves 2

15 ml/1 tablespoon currants
15 ml/1 tablespoon sherry or
  lukewarm water
30 ml/2 tablespoons soured cream
30 ml/2 tablespoons single cream
30 ml/2 tablespoons sherry vinegar
200 g/7 oz celery
1 tart eating apple
1 large ripe avocado
15 ml/1 tablespoon chopped
  fresh parsley
25 g/1 oz walnuts, coarsely chopped
sea salt and freshly ground
  white pepper

Approximately per portion:
2,000 kj/480 kcal
7 g protein
42 g fat
17 g carbohydrate
2 g fibre

● Approximate preparation
  time: 20 minutes

1. Put the currants in a bowl
and pour in the sherry or
lukewarm water. Cover and set
aside to soak until the currants
have plumped up.

2. Beat the soured cream with the
single cream and vinegar. Season to
taste with salt and pepper. Cover
and set aside in the refrigerator
until required.

3. Cut the celery sticks into thin
strips. Quarter and core the apple
and cut it into thin slices. Thinly
peel the avocado, cut it in half
lengthways and remove the stone.

Dice the flesh. Put the celery,
apple and avocado into a serving
bowl. Drain the currants.

4. Add the parsley, half the walnuts
and the currants to the salad. Pour
in the dressing, toss lightly to mix
and scatter the remaining walnuts
on top to garnish.

Cauliflower and tomato salad

Quick • Easy

Serves 2

50 ml/2 fl oz natural yogurt
50 ml/2 fl oz single cream
2.5 ml/$^1/_2$ teaspoon Dijon mustard
30 ml/2 tablespoons lemon juice
30 ml/2 tablespoons mayonnaise,
  preferably home-made
15 ml/1 tablespoon chopped fresh
  mixed dill and parsley
300 g/11 oz cauliflower
2 ripe, firm tomatoes, sliced
50 g/2 oz lamb's lettuce
sea salt

Approximately per portion:
1,100 kj/260 kcal
7 g protein
23 g fat
11 g carbohydrate
7 g fibre

● Approximate preparation
  time: 30 minutes

1. Beat the yogurt with the cream
in a large bowl. Stir in the mustard,
lemon juice, mayonnaise, herbs
and a pinch of salt.

2. Cut the cauliflower into thin
slices. Cut the tender green inner

leaves into thin strips. Add them to
the dressing and toss to coat. Pile
the salad on to the centre of two
serving plates.

3. Arrange the tomatoes around
the cauliflower and put the lamb's
lettuce between the tomato slices.
Serve immediately.

Tip

Serve salads as fresh as possible.
Always prepare the dressing
first and keep it, covered, in the
refrigerator. Just before serving,
wash and trim the vegetables,
lettuce and herbs. If necessary,
wrap them in a damp cloth and
store them in the refrigerator –
but for only a short time. Only
chop or slice the ingredients at
the last minute and mix
immediately with the dressing
or arrange them on serving
plates and pour the dressing
over them.

Above: Avocado salad with celery
Below: Cauliflower and tomato salad

Sauerkraut with rye sprouts

Quick

Serves 2
300 g/11 oz sauerkraut, drained
    and chopped
115 g/4 oz beetroot
30 ml/2 tablespoons sunflower oil
1 small yellow pepper, seeded and
    cut into strips
30 ml/2 tablespoons rye sprouts

Approximately per portion:
760 kj/180 kcal
8 g protein
12 g fat
11 g carbohydrate
6 g fibre

● Approximate preparation
   time: 10 minutes

1. Place the sauerkraut in a bowl. Coarsely grate the beetroot into the sauerkraut and stir in the sunflower oil. Arrange the salad on two serving plates.

2. Arrange the pepper strips around the salad and put 15 ml/ 1 tablespoon of the rye sprouts in the middle of each plate.

Variation
You can easily adapt this salad. Mix 30 ml/2 tablespoons soured cream, 1–2 thinly sliced carrots and 1 small chopped orange into the sauerkraut. Sprinkle the salad with cress.

Greek-style beans

Rather time-consuming

Serves 2
250 ml/8 fl oz water
1/4 vegetable stock cube
6 fresh thyme sprigs
250 g/9 oz green beans, sliced
30 ml/2 tablespoons red
    wine vinegar
15 ml/1 tablespoon cider vinegar
30 ml/2 tablespoons extra virgin
    olive oil
15 ml/1 tablespoon sunflower oil
1 red onion, finely chopped
115 g/4 oz fennel
1 yellow pepper, seeded and cut
    into thin strips
150 g/5 oz ripe, firm
    tomatoes, diced
30 ml/2 tablespoons chopped
    fresh mixed herbs, such as
    basil, thyme, dill and tarragon
75 g/3 oz feta cheese
sea salt and freshly ground
    black pepper

Approximately per portion:
1,400 kj/330 kcal
12 g protein
24 g fat
17 g carbohydrate
10 g fibre

● Approximate preparation
   time: 40 minutes

1. Bring the water to the boil in a medium saucepan and add the vegetable stock cube and thyme. Add the beans, bring back to the boil, cover and simmer over a medium heat for 10–15 minutes, until they are tender, but still firm to bite.

2. Meanwhile, make the vinaigrette. Beat the red wine vinegar with the cider vinegar and salt and pepper to taste. Beat in the olive and sunflower oils, a tablespoon at a time.

3. Put the onion in a bowl and pour the vinaigrette over it. Drain the beans and add them to the bowl. Cut the fennel in half and then into thin strips. Add the fennel to the bowl with the yellow pepper and tomatoes.

4. Sprinkle the herbs over the salad. Toss lightly to mix and season to taste with salt and pepper. Crumble the feta on top and set aside for about 10 minutes for the flavours to mingle.

Variation
You could also make this salad with fresh broad beans. Very young beans – pods no longer than 7.5 cm/3 inches – can simply be trimmed and sliced before cooking in boiling water or stock until tender. Larger beans must be shelled and older beans should be skinned as well.

Above: Sauerkraut with rye sprouts
Below: Greek-style beans

Fresh vegetable mix with sprouting seeds

Begin in advance

Serves 2
60–90 ml/4–6 tablespoons barley
  or rye grain
30 ml/2 tablespoons
  sunflower seeds
1 eating apple
115 g/4 oz carrots
115 g/4 oz celeriac
15 ml/1 tablespoon chopped fresh
  lemon balm
175 ml/6 fl oz Greek-style yogurt
15 ml/1 tablespoon lemon juice

Approximately per portion:
1,000 kj/240 kcal
10 g protein
9 g fat
31 g carbohydrate
9 g fibre

● Approximate preparation
  time: 20 minutes, plus
  sprouting time

1. Rinse the grain in cold water and put it to sprout 2–3 days before you plan to make the vegetable mix (see page 7).

2. Dry-fry the sunflower seeds in a heavy-based frying pan over a medium heat, stirring frequently, until golden and beginning to give off their aroma. Remove the pan from the heat and set aside.

3. Quarter and core the apple and grate it coarsely into a bowl. Finely grate the carrots and celeriac into the bowl. Stir in the sprouting grain.

4. Stir in the lemon balm, yogurt and lemon juice. Scatter over the toasted sunflower seeds to garnish.

Raw grain muesli

Easy

A raw grain muesli is the ideal breakfast, as the fibre in the uncooked grain make you feel full for a long while and the carbohydrate provides a steady release of energy.

Serves 2
60–90 ml/4–6 tablespoons wheat
  or other cereal grains
  (except oats)
90–120 ml/6–8 tablespoons water
90–120 ml/6–8 tablespoons milk or
  natural yogurt
30–45 ml/2–3 tablespoons
  single cream
15 ml/1 tablespoon finely chopped
  hazelnuts or almonds or 15 ml/
  1 tablespoon sunflower seeds
200 g/7 oz strawberries or other
  berries, halved or chopped
1 banana, thinly sliced
1 eating apple, thinly sliced

Approximately per portion:
1,400 kj/330 kcal
8 g protein
12 g fat
47 g carbohydrate
10 g fibre

● Approximate preparation
  time: 15 minutes, plus soaking
  time

1. Coarsely crush the grains and place in a bowl. Stir in sufficient water to make a thick paste. Cover and set aside at room temperature (10–20°C/50–68°F) overnight or for up to 10 hours.

2. Stir the milk or yogurt, the cream and nuts or seeds into the cereal paste.

3. Stir the berries, banana and apple into the cereal mixture and serve the muesli immediately.

Tip

Instead of using water, you can soak the grains in soured cream, crème fraîche or live yogurt because the bacteria in these dairy products kills germs. You should never soak grains in fresh milk because this would produce an ideal breeding-ground for bacteria. In winter, muesli is more digestible if eaten slightly warm. So while you are preparing it, set the bowl over warm water and, if necessary, warm the milk slightly before adding it.

Above: Raw grain muesli
Below: Fresh vegetable mix with sprouting seeds

Onion toast

Easy • Quick

This hearty onion spread also goes well with potatoes boiled in their skins or baked in their jackets or serve it as an accompaniment to spicy patties.

Serves 2
40 g/1¹/2 oz butter
4 slices wholemeal bread
150 g/5 oz onions, halved
*   and sliced*
115 g/4 oz Harvarti or Caerphilly
*   cheese, finely diced*
1.5 ml/¹/4 teaspoon
*   ground coriander*
1.5 ml/¹/4 teaspoon
*   ground fenugreek*
1.5 ml/¹/4 teaspoon paprika
1.5 ml/¹/4 teaspoon herb salt
¹/4 red pepper, seeded and cut into
*   thin strips*
¹/4 green pepper, seeded and cut
*   into thin strips*
¹/4 yellow pepper, seeded and cut
*   into thin strips*
mixed salad leaves, dressed with
*   herb vinaigrette, to serve*

Approximately per portion:
2,000 kj/480 kcal
19 g protein
34 g fat
26 g carbohydrate
5 g fibre

● Approximate preparation
   time: 25 minutes

1. Melt half the butter in a large, heavy-based frying pan. Fry the bread slices on both sides over a medium heat, in batches if necessary. Remove from the pan and set aside.

2. Melt the remaining butter in the pan and fry the onions over a medium heat, stirring occasionally, for about 5 minutes, until golden. Remove the pan from the heat.

3. Stir the cheese into the onions. Add the coriander, fenugreek, paprika and herb salt and mix well.

4. Spread the onion mixture evenly over the fried bread. Arrange the pepper strips in a lattice pattern on top.

5. Toast under a preheated grill or fry in a covered frying pan for a few more minutes, until the cheese has melted. Serve immediately with mixed salad leaves, dressed with herb vinaigrette.

Emmental cheese slices

Easy

Makes 4 slices
1 small garlic clove, finely chopped
75 g/3 oz Emmental cheese,
*   freshly grated*
1 tablespoon finely chopped
*   fresh parsley*
1 egg, lightly beaten
1.5 ml/¹/4 teaspoon
*   ground fenugreek*
1.5 ml/¹/4 teaspoon freshly
*   grated nutmeg*
1.5 ml/¹/4 teaspoon freshly ground
*   white pepper*
4 slices wholemeal bread
25 g/1 oz butter
herb salt
fresh basil or thyme leaves,
*   to garnish*
salad, to serve

Approximately per slice:
930 kj/220 kcal
10 g protein
13 g fat
17 g carbohydrate
2 g fibre

● Approximate preparation
   time: 20 minutes

1. Mix together the garlic, grated cheese, parsley and beaten egg. Stir in the fenugreek, nutmeg and pepper and season to taste with herb salt.

2. Spread the cheese mixture on the bread slices.

3. Melt the butter in a large, heavy-based frying pan. Add the bread slices with the cheese topping downwards. Cover and fry over a low heat for 5 minutes, until the cheese is golden yellow. Cook in batches, if necessary.

4. Sprinkle the cheese slices with basil or thyme leaves and serve immediately with a salad.

Above: Emmental cheese slices
Below: Onion toast

Onion and nut spread

Exquisite

This delicious spread will keep in the refrigerator for about 8 days.

Makes about 300 g/11 oz
115 g/4 oz butter
115 g/4 oz onions, finely chopped
2 garlic cloves, finely chopped
75 g/3 oz hazelnuts
7.5 ml/1 1/2 teaspoons
  dried marjoram
5 ml/1 teaspoon dried thyme
1/4 bay leaf
1 teaspoon chilli powder
15 ml/1 tablespoon yeast extract
10 ml/2 teaspoons mushroom stock
  or mushroom ketchup
90 ml/6 tablespoons water
sea salt and freshly ground
  white pepper

**Approximately per
100 g/3¾ oz:**
2,000 kj/470 kcal
9 g protein
45 g fat
10 g carbohydrate
3 g fibre

● Approximate preparation
  time: 1 1/2–2 1/2 hours

---

1. Melt 40 g/1 1/2 oz of the butter in a frying pan. Fry the onions and garlic over a medium heat, stirring occasionally, until golden.

2. Meanwhile, process the nuts and herbs in a food processor until finely chopped.

3. Add the nut mixture and chilli powder to the onions and fry, stirring constantly, for 1–2 minutes.

4. Remove the pan from the heat and stir in the yeast extract, mushroom stock or ketchup, water and the remaining butter.

5. Season to taste with salt and pepper, then cover and set aside in the refrigerator for 1–2 hours. Serve at room temperature.

Dried fruit spread

Rather time-consuming

This spread will keep in the refrigerator for about 2 weeks.

Makes about 400 g/14 oz
250 g/9 oz mixed dried fruits, such
  as pears, prunes or apricots and
  apples, chopped
250 ml/8 fl oz apple juice
grated rind of 1/2 lemon
cinnamon, lemon juice or pear
  juice (optional)

**Approximately per
100 g/3³/4 oz:**
775 kj/185 kcal
2 g protein
1 g fat
42 g carbohydrate
5 g fibre

● Approximate preparation
  time: 15 minutes, plus soaking

---

1. Put the dried fruit into a bowl, pour in the apple juice and set aside to soak for about 6 hours.

2. Drain the fruit, reserving the soaking liquid. Place the fruit in a food processor and process to a purée. Add the lemon rind and

enough of the soaking liquid to give a spreading consistency. Season the spread with cinnamon, lemon juice or pear juice, if wished.

Savoury cheese cream

Quick

This tasty spread will keep in the refrigerator for 3–4 days

Makes 150 g/5 oz
50 g/2 oz butter
105 ml/7 tablespoons curd cheese
10 ml/2 teaspoons yeast extract
2.5 ml/1/2 teaspoon herb salt
3.75 ml/3/4 teaspoon
  ground fenugreek

**Approximately per
150 g/5 oz:**
2,400 kj/570 kcal
14 g protein
53 g fat
5 g carbohydrate
0 g fibre

● Approximate preparation
  time: 5 minutes

---

1. Put the butter into a heatproof bowl and set it over a bowl of warm water until just melting.

2. Remove from the heat and beat in the curd cheese and yeast extract. Season with the salt and ground fenugreek.

Above: Onion and nut spread
Centre Savoury cheese cream
Below: Dried fruit spread

Cucumber soup with dill

Quick

Serves 2
30 ml/2 tablespoons sunflower oil
150 ml/¼ pint vegetable stock
     or water
5 shallots, finely chopped
115 g/4 oz floury potatoes,
     finely diced
1 vegetable stock cube
4 fresh rosemary needles, chopped
400 g/14 oz cucumber
75 ml/5 tablespoons crème fraîche
15 ml/1 tablespoon chopped
     fresh borage
30 ml/2 tablespoons chopped
     fresh dill
5 ml/1 teaspoon lemon juice
sea salt and freshly ground
     white pepper

To garnish:
dill flowers
borage flowers

Approximately per portion:
1,400 kj/330 kcal
4 g protein
27 g fat
18 g carbohydrate
5 g fibre

● Approximate preparation
   time: 30 minutes

1. Heat the sunflower oil and
15 ml/1 tablespoon of the stock or
water in a heavy-based saucepan.
Add the shallots and potatoes and
cook over a medium heat, stirring
occasionally, for about 5 minutes,
until golden.

2. Add the remaining vegetable
stock or water, the stock cube and

rosemary. Cover and simmer
over a medium heat for about
5 minutes.

3. Meanwhile, peel the cucumber,
halve it lengthways and scoop out
the seeds. Cut the flesh into
1–2 cm/½–¾ inch cubes. Add the
cucumber to the potatoes, cover
and cook for about 10 minutes
over a low heat.

4. Purée the mixture with a hand-
held electric mixer or process in a
food processor and then return to
the pan. Stir in the crème fraîche,
borage, dill and lemon juice and
heat through gently. Season to
taste with salt and pepper.

5. Ladle the soup into warm
bowls, sprinkle a few dill and
borage flowers on top and serve.

Vegetable and millet soup

Easy

Serves 2
350 g/12 oz mixed vegetables,
     such as carrots, celery and
     Savoy cabbage
500 ml/18 fl oz water
150 g/5 oz millet
30 ml/2 tablespoons vegetable
     stock granules
2 chopped fresh lovage leaves
200 g/7 oz ripe tomatoes,
     finely chopped
5 ml/1 teaspoon dried marjoram
20 g/¾ oz butter
30 ml/2 tablespoons chopped
     fresh parsley
freshly grated Parmesan cheese, to
     serve (optional)

Approximately per portion:
1,700 kj/400 kcal
12 g protein
12 g fat
61 g carbohydrate
11 g fibre

● Approximate preparation
   time: 40 minutes

1. Prepare the vegetables. Finely
chop carrots and cut celery and
cabbage into strips.

2. Bring the water to the boil in a
large saucepan. Rinse the millet
under cold running water.

3. Add the millet, vegetables, stock
granules and lovage to the pan,
cover and simmer over a low heat
for 10–12 minutes.

4. Add the tomatoes and
marjoram to the pan, cover and
simmer for a further 3–4 minutes.
Stir in the butter and parsley.

5. Ladle the soup into warm bowls
and serve sprinkled with grated
cheese, if liked.

Above: Cucumber soup with dill
Below: Vegetable and millet soup

Lentil stew with tomatoes

Easy

Lentils cook quicker if you soak them overnight, as in the following recipe, but this is not essential. If the lentils are not soaked, the cooking time is lengthened by about 30 minutes.

Serves 2
150 g/5 oz lentils
40 g/1¹/₂ oz cornmeal
¹/₂ bay leaf
115 g/4 oz leeks, cut into thin strips
2 vegetable stock cubes
150 g/5 oz ripe tomatoes, chopped
15 ml/1 tablespoon chopped
    fresh marjoram
5 ml/1 teaspoon fresh thyme leaves
15 g/¹/₂ oz butter
90 ml/6 tablespoons single cream
15 ml/1 tablespoon dry white
    wine (optional)
1 small garlic clove
5–10 ml/1–2 teaspoons lemon juice
30 ml/2 tablespoons chopped
    fresh parsley

Approximately per portion:
2,000 kj/480 kcal
22 g protein
19 g fat
57 g carbohydrate
11 g fibre

● Approximate preparation
  time: 30 minutes, plus soaking.

1. Rinse the lentils in a sieve under cold running water. Pour them and the cornmeal into 750 ml/4 pints water. Add the bay leaf and set aside to soak for at least 6 hours or overnight.

2. Pour the lentils, cornmeal and the soaking water into a saucepan and bring to the boil. Add the leek strips and stock cubes. Cover and simmer over a low heat for about 10 minutes.

3. Put the tomatoes into a food processor and process to a purée. Stir them into the lentils with the marjoram and thyme.

4. Remove the saucepan from the heat. Remove and discard the bay leaf. Stir in the butter, cream, wine, if using, garlic and lemon juice to taste. Transfer to serving plates and sprinkle with the parsley.

Potato and mushroom soup

Exquisite

Serves 2

115 g/4 oz leeks
150 g/5 oz floury potatoes
475 ml/16 fl oz water
15 ml/1 tablespoon vegetable
   stock granules
7.5 ml/1 1/2 teaspoon fresh
   thyme leaves
2 chopped fresh lovage leaves
115 g/4 oz small button mushrooms
3.75 ml/3/4 teaspoon mushroom
   stock or mushroom ketchup
25 g/1 oz butter
30 ml/2 tablespoons chopped
   fresh parsley
freshly ground black pepper
30 ml/2 tablespoons crème fraîche,
   to garnish

Approximately per portion:
1,200 kj/285 kcal
5 g protein
23 g fat
15 g carbohydrate
5 g fibre

● Approximate preparation
  time: 35 minutes

Tip

Soups and sauces taste even better with home-made stock. Simmer 500 g/1 1/4 lb chopped mixed vegetables, such as carrots, leeks, celery and onions, 1 fresh parsley sprig, 1 fresh lovage leaf and 1 bay leaf in 1 litre/1 3/4 pints water over a low heat for 30 minutes. Strain before using.

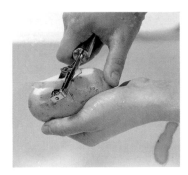

1. Trim the leeks and cut them lengthways into thin strips. Peel the potatoes thinly.

2. Bring the water to the boil in a large saucepan and add the stock granules, leeks, thyme and lovage. Grate the potatoes into the boiling stock. Cover and simmer over a medium heat for about 8 minutes, until the potatoes are tender, but still firm to bite.

3. Slice the mushrooms, stir them into the soup and simmer for 2–3 minutes.

4. Remove the saucepan from the heat. Stir in the mushroom stock or ketchup, butter and parsley. Season the soup with pepper to taste and ladle it into warm soup plates. Swirl 15 ml/1 tablespoon crème fraîche in the middle of each plate and serve.

Onion soup with spelt

Quick • Easy

Serves 2
20 g/³/4 oz butter
250 g/9 oz onions, thinly sliced
600 ml/1 pint water
75 g/3 oz spelt
1 vegetable stock cube
115 g/4 oz g mild blue-veined
    cheese, such as dolcelatte, diced
30 ml/2 tablespoons crème fraîche
freshly ground black pepper
30 ml/2 tablespoons snipped fresh
    chives, to garnish

Approximately per portion:
2,400 kj/570 kcal
19 g protein
39 g fat
34 g carbohydrate
8 g fibre
● Approximate preparation time: 30 minutes

1. Melt the butter in a large, heavy-based saucepan. Add the onions and fry over a medium heat, stirring occasionally, for about 5 minutes, until golden brown.

2. Add the water and the spelt grains, bring to the boil and simmer over a low heat for about 10 minutes. Add the stock cube and turn off the heat, but leave the saucepan on the hob for a further 10 minutes.

3. Add the cheese and stir until it has melted. Stir in the crème fraîche. Season the soup with pepper to taste, ladle into warm bowls and sprinkle the chives on top. Serve immediately.

Crushed barley soup with vegetables

Easy

This hearty soup also tastes excellent made with green spelt grains, rice, wheat, cornmeal, millet or buckwheat. Choose whatever vegetables are in season.

Serves 2
600 ml/1 pint hot water
50 g/2 oz barley, very
    coarsely crushed
22.5 ml/4¹/2 teaspoons vegetable
    stock granules
200 g/7 oz mixed vegetables,
    such as leeks, carrots and
    Brussels sprouts
45 ml/3 tablespoons single cream
45 ml/3 tablespoons soured cream
10 ml/2 teaspoons lemon juice
60 ml/3 tablespoons chopped
    fresh mixed herbs, such as
    marjoram, parsley, chives
    and lovage
1.5–2.5 ml/¹/4–¹/2 teaspoon
    chilli powder

Approximately per portion:
920 kj/220 kcal
9 g protein
10 g fat
22 g carbohydrate
7 g fibre
● Approximate preparation time: 30 minutes

1. Pour the water into a large saucepan and add the crushed barley and stock granules. Stir well to mix, then cover and set aside to soak while you prepare the vegetables.

2. Finely chop the vegetables. Bring the water in the pan to the boil, then add the vegetables. Cover and simmer over a low heat for about 5 minutes, until all the vegetables are tender, but still firm to bite.

3. Stir in the cream, soured cream, lemon juice and mixed herbs and season to taste with chilli powder. Serve immediately.

Tip

The soup will be even more nutritious if you chop the vegetables in a food processor and add them raw to the finished soup.

*Above: Crushed barley soup with vegetables
Below: Onion soup with spelt*

Oat slices with a cheese and nut crust

Exquisite • Easy

Serves 2
150 g/5 oz oats
200 ml/7 fl oz water
1 vegetable stock cube
150 g/5 oz mixed vegetables, such
*   as leeks, celery and carrots*
3 celery leaves
handful of fresh parsley
2 eggs, separated
60 ml/4 tablespoons single cream
15 g/¹/2 oz butter
50 g/2 oz walnuts or hazelnuts,
*   coarsely chopped*
10 ml/2 teaspoons dried thyme
5 ml/1 teaspoon dried marjoram
2.5 ml/¹/2 teaspoon
*   ground fenugreek*
sunflower oil, for brushing
40 g/1¹/2 oz freshly grated
*   Parmesan cheese*
2.5 ml/¹/2 teaspoon chilli powder
herb salt
salad or grilled mushrooms, to serve

Approximately per portion:
3,300 kj/790 kcal
28 g protein
52 g fat
54 g carbohydrate
7 g fibre

● Approximate preparation
   time: 1¹/2 hours

1. Dry-fry the oats in a heavy-based frying pan over a low heat, stirring frequently, for about 20–30 minutes. Set aside to cool. Bring the water to the boil, add the oats and the stock cube. Cover, turn off the heat and leave them to soak on the hob.

2. Finely chop the vegetables with the celery leaves and parsley in a food processor. Stir them into the oatmeal. Add the egg yolks, cream, butter, 90 ml/6 tablespoons of the nuts, the thyme, marjoram and fenugreek. Season to taste with the salt.

3. Pre-heat the oven to 200°C/ 400°F/Gas 6 and brush a loose-based 25 cm/10 inch cake tin with oil. Beat the egg whites until stiff, then fold them into the oatmeal mixture. Spoon the mixture into the tin and smooth the surface. Mix the cheese, the remaining nuts and the chilli powder and spread evenly over the oatmeal mixture, pressing down lightly.

4. Bake for 30 minutes, until golden brown. Remove from the tin and serve with salad or freshly grilled mushrooms.

Greek risotto

Easy

Serves 2
150 g/5 oz long-grain brown rice
1 bay leaf
300 ml/^{1}/$_2$ pint unsalted vegetable
   stock or water
1 vegetable stock cube
2 medium onions
1 garlic clove
30 ml/2 tablespoons extra virgin
   olive oil
10 g/^{1}/$_4$ oz butter
1 medium green pepper, seeded
   and cut into strips
1 medium yellow pepper, seeded
   and cut into strips
^{1}/$_4$ dried red chilli, seeded, or pinch
   of cayenne pepper
5–10 ml/1–2 teaspoons
   dried thyme
5 ml/1 teaspoon dried oregano
200 g/7 oz ripe tomatoes, chopped
115 g/4 oz feta cheese
15 ml/1 tablespoon fresh
   basil leaves
sea salt

Approximately per portion:
1,700 kj/400 kcal
17 g protein
26 g fat
54 g carbohydrate
8 g fibre

● Approximate preparation
   time: 45 minutes, plus soaking

Tip

If you do not have time to
soak the rice, you can still
cook the dish. Simply double
the cooking time.

1. Rinse the rice in a sieve under cold running water and place in a large saucepan. Add the bay leaf and vegetable stock and set aside to soak for 30 minutes. Bring to the boil, cover and simmer over a medium heat for 20 minutes. Crumble in the stock cube and remove and discard the bay leaf.

2. Meanwhile, quarter the onions and thinly slice. Finely chop the garlic. Heat 15 ml/1 tablespoon of the olive oil, the butter and 15 ml/1 tablespoon water in a heavy-based frying pan. Add the onions and garlic and cook over a low heat, stirring occasionally, for about 10 minutes.

3. Add the green and yellow pepper strips, chilli or cayenne, thyme and oregano to the onions and cook for a further 1–2 minutes. Stir in the rice and season to taste with salt.

4. Sprinkle the tomatoes over the rice. Crumble the cheese over them and drizzle with the remaining olive oil. Cover and set aside for about 5 minutes to allow the flavours to infuse. Sprinkle with the basil and serve.

Green spelt grain in a vegetable ring

Easy

Because of its spicy taste, green spelt grain is the ideal cereal for newcomers to wholefood cooking. You can vary the vegetables according to the season.

Serves 2

150 g/5 oz green spelt grain
250 ml/8 fl oz water
15 ml/1 tablespoon vegetable
    stock granules
500 g/1¼ lb mixed vegetables,
    such as leeks, Savoy cabbage
    or Brussels sprouts, carrots
    and celeriac
15 ml/1 tablespoon sunflower oil
1 medium onion, roughly chopped
10 ml/2 teaspoons mushroom stock
    or mushroom ketchup
1 ripe tomato, diced
15 ml/1 tablespoon fresh marjoram
    or 2.5 ml/½ teaspoon dried
2 tablespoons crème fraîche
15 ml/1 tablespoon chopped parsley
20 g/¾ oz butter

Approximately per portion:
2,300 kj/550 kcal
17 g protein
26 g fat
63 g carbohydrate
5 g fibre

● Approximate preparation
    time: 40 minutes, plus soaking

1. Rinse the green spelt grain in a sieve under cold running water. Tip it into a saucepan, add the water and set aside to soak for 6–10 hours or overnight.

2. Bring the water in the pan to the boil and simmer for about 10 minutes. Stir in the vegetable stock granules. Cover, turn off the heat and leave on the hob for 10–15 minutes.

3. Meanwhile, prepare the vegetables. Cut leeks and cabbage into thin strips. Trim Brussels sprouts and cut a cross in the bases. Coarsely grate carrots and celeriac.

4. Heat the sunflower oil in a flameproof casserole and fry the onion over a low heat, stirring occasionally, for 5 minutes, until soft and translucent.

5. Add the prepared vegetables, mushroom stock or ketchup and 60–75 ml/4–5 tablespoons water. Cover and simmer over a medium heat for 8–10 minutes.

6. Stir in the tomato and simmer for a further 2 minutes. Stir in the marjoram and crème fraîche.

7. Stir the parsley and butter into the green spelt grain. Push the

---

vegetables into a ring around the edge of the casserole and heap the green spelt grain in the middle. Alternatively, arrange the vegetables around the edge of a serving dish and heap the green spelt grain in the middle. Serve immediately.

Tip

Try green spelt grain as an accompaniment to fried mushrooms. It tastes exquisite if you mix in chopped toasted hazelnuts or sunflower seeds.

Green spelt grain is very aromatic and is the perfect partner for the strong flavour of the vegetables.

Green spelt grain patties

Ideal for a picnic or packed lunch

These hearty cereal cakes also taste wonderful cold. Spread them with a little butter and top with a mild cheese.

Serves 2
115 g/4 oz green spelt grains
40 g/1¹/2 oz buckwheat
200 ml/7 fl oz water
7.5 ml/1¹/2 teaspoons vegetable
  stock granules
1 small onion, finely chopped
45 ml/3 tablespoons single cream
1 egg, lightly beaten
3.75 ml/³/4 teaspoon
  dried marjoram
30 ml/2 tablespoons chopped
  fresh parsley
pinch of freshly grated nutmeg
25 g/1 oz hazelnuts, finely ground
30 ml/2 tablespoons sunflower oil
sea salt and freshly ground
  white pepper
braised vegetables and salad,
  to serve

Approximately per portion:
2,500 kj/600 kcal
13 g protein
37 g fat
52 g carbohydrate
7 g fibre
● Approximate preparation time: 50 minutes

1. Coarsely crush the green spelt grains, then mix them with the buckwheat, vegetable stock granules and water. Bring to the boil over a very low heat, turn off the heat and leave for about 15 minutes, until all the liquid has been absorbed. It is not usually necessary to stir it.

2. Uncover the grain mixture to allow the steam to escape. Stir in the onion, cream, egg, marjoram and parsley, then stir in the nutmeg and season to taste with salt and pepper. Set aside to cool.

3. Form the mixture into little patties and roll them in the nuts. Heat the oil in a heavy-based frying pan and fry the patties until golden brown on both sides. Serve with braised vegetables and salad.

Variation
Green spelt grains may be difficult to obtain; try using the more readily available bulgur wheat.

Spicy corn soufflé

For guests

Serves 4
300 g/11 oz coarse cornmeal
750 ml/1¹/4 pints water
1 vegetable stock cube
3.75 ml/³/4 teaspoon curry powder
5 ml/1 teaspoon dried marjoram
25 g/1 oz butter, plus extra
  for greasing
1 leek, cut into strips
3 eggs, separated
150 g/5 oz Emmental cheese,
  freshly grated

To serve:
tomato sauce
Celery with crème fraîche
  (see page 42)

Approximately per portion:
2,200 kj/520 kcal
22 g protein
23 g fat
57 g carbohydrate
1 g fibre
● Approximate preparation time: 1 hour 20 minutes

1. Put the cornmeal and water into a saucepan and mix well together. Crumble in the stock cube, add the curry powder and marjoram, bring to the boil and simmer for about 2 minutes. Turn off the heat, but leave the saucepan on the hob for about 20 minutes. If any liquid has still not been absorbed, drain it off.

2. Meanwhile, grease a soufflé dish with a little butter. Preheat the oven to 200°C/400°F/Gas 6.

3. Stir the leek, butter, egg yolks and 115 g/4 oz of the cheese into the cornmeal mixture.

4. Whisk the egg whites until stiff, then fold them into the mixture. Spoon the mixture into the prepared dish and sprinkle the remaining cheese on top.

5. Bake the soufflé for 40–45 minutes, until it is well risen and the top is golden brown. Serve with tomato sauce and celery with crème fraîche.

Above: Green spelt grain patties
Below: Spicy corn soufflé

Onion and nut rice

Easy

Serves 2
130 g/4¹/2 oz long grain brown rice
250 ml/8 fl oz water
¹/2 bay leaf
10 ml/2 teaspoons vegetable
    stock granules
25 g/1 oz butter
115 g/4 oz onions, quartered and
    cut into strips
1 garlic clove, finely chopped
50 g/2 oz hazelnuts,
    roughly chopped
2.5 ml/¹/2 teaspoon curry powder
pinch of cayenne pepper
sea salt
Celery with crème fraîche (see
    page 42), Savoy cabbage, Brussels
    sprouts or scorzonera, to serve

Approximately per portion:
1,400 kj/330 kcal
9 g protein
26 g fat
41 g carbohydrate
4 g fibre
● Approximate preparation   time: 35 minutes, plus soaking

1. Put the rice in a saucepan, pour in the water and add the bay leaf. Set aside to soak overnight.

2. Bring the rice to the boil and simmer over a low heat for about 20 minutes. Stir in the vegetable stock granules, turn of the heat, but leave the pan to stand on the hob for about 10 minutes. Remove and discard the bay leaf.

3. Meanwhile, melt the butter in a frying pan. Add the onions and fry over a medium heat, stirring occasionally, for 5 minutes, until golden brown. Stir in the garlic, nuts and curry powder and fry for a further 2–3 minutes.

4. Stir the onion mixture into the rice and season to taste with cayenne and salt. Serve immediately with celery with crème fraîche, Savoy cabbage, Brussels sprouts or scorzonera.

Rye groats with sunflower seeds

Quick

Serves 2
130 g/4¹/2 oz rye, very
    coarsely crushed
¹/2 bay leaf
7.5 ml/1¹/2 teaspoons vegetable
    stock granules
250 ml/8 fl oz water
60 ml/4 tablespoons
    sunflower seeds
5 ml/1 teaspoon fresh thyme leaves
15 g/¹/2 oz butter, diced
15 ml/1 tablespoon chopped
    fresh parsley

Approximately per portion:
1,400 kj/330 kcal
11 g protein
17 g fat
36 g carbohydrate
10 g fibre
● Approximate preparation   time: 30 minutes

1. Put the rye into a saucepan, add the bay leaf and stock granules and pour in the water. Bring to the boil, cover and simmer over a very low heat, stirring constantly, for 10–20 minutes. If necessary, add another 15–30 ml/1–2 tablespoons water. Turn off the heat, but leave the saucepan on the hob for a further 10–20 minutes.

2. Meanwhile, dry-fry the sunflower seeds in a heavy-based frying pan over a medium heat, stirring frequently, until golden and fragrant.

3. Uncover the rye mixture to allow the steam to escape. Lightly stir in the thyme and butter with a fork. Finally, add the toasted sunflower seeds and chopped parsley. Serve immediately.

Tip

You can also prepare barley, spelt, wheat, green spelt grain and buckwheat using this recipe. (Do not crush buckwheat.)

Above: Onion and nut rice
Below: Rye groats with sunflower seeds

Leek and onion tart with peanuts

For guests • Rather time-consuming

Makes 1 x 25 cm/10 inch tart
150 ml/¹/4 pint lukewarm buttermilk
15 g/¹/2 oz fresh yeast
175 g/6 fl oz plain wholemeal flour,
 plus extra for dusting
75 g/3 oz rye flour
5 ml/1 teaspoon caraway seeds,
 finely ground
5 ml/1 teaspoon coriander seeds,
 finely ground
25 g/1 oz butter, softened
25 g/1 oz Parmesan cheese,
 freshly grated
sea salt

For the filling:
200 g/7 oz onions
200 g/7 oz leeks
25 g/1 oz butter
30 ml/2 tablespoons water
1 vegetable stock cube
2.5 ml/¹/2 teaspoon chilli powder
5 ml/1 teaspoon dried marjoram
10 ml/2 teaspoons fresh
 thyme leaves
sunflower oil, for brushing
150 g/5 oz Emmental cheese, grated
2 eggs
120–150 ml/4–5 fl oz crème fraîche
75 g/3 oz roasted peanuts
salt and freshly ground black
 pepper

Approximately per slice:
1,700 kj/400 kcal
15 g protein
27 g fat
24 g carbohydrate
5 g fibre

● Approximate preparation
 time: 2 hours 10 minutes

1. Pour the buttermilk into a small bowl and crumble in the yeast. Sift the flours and the ground spices into a large bowl and tip in any bran from the sieve. Make a well in the centre and add the yeast mixture. Mix about two-thirds of the flour mixture into the yeast mixture. Mix in the butter, 2.5 ml/¹/2 teaspoon salt and the cheese. Mix in the remaining flour mixture.

2. Knead with an electric mixer fitted with dough hooks for about 10 minutes, until medium soft. Set aside in a warm place for 30–40 minutes, until it has nearly doubled in bulk.

3. Meanwhile, prepare the filling. Halve the onions and then cut them into thin strips. Cut the leeks in half lengthways and then into 1 cm/¹/2 inch wide strips.

4. Melt the butter in a frying pan and fry the onions over a low heat, stirring occasionally, for 5 minutes. Add the leeks and the water and crumble in the stock cube. Cover and simmer over a medium heat until the vegetables are just tender. Stir in the chilli powder and herbs and season well with pepper.

5. Brush a loose-based 25 cm/ 10 inch cake tin with sunflower oil. Preheat the oven to 200°C/400°F/ Gas 6. Turn out the pastry on to a lightly floured surface and knead briefly. Roll it out and line the prepared tin.

6. Scatter half the cheese evenly over the base of the pastry case. Spoon in the leek and onion mixture and scatter the remaining cheese on top.

7. Whisk the eggs with the crème fraîche and a pinch of salt. Pour them into the pastry case and scatter the peanuts on top.

8. Bake the tart for about 40–45 minutes, until the topping is golden brown. Serve hot or cold.

Variation

For Crispy cheese rolls, make the dough as described and form into rolls. Set aside on a baking sheet to rise for about 10 minutes. Brush with water or beaten egg and, if desired, sprinkle with sesame, poppy, caraway, sunflower or pumpkin seeds and gently press them in. Bake the rolls in a pre-heated oven at 200°C/400°F/ Gas 6 for about 35 minutes, until golden brown.

Tip

The leek tart is suitable for freezing. To serve, bake it for 20 minutes in a preheated oven at 150°F/300°F/Gas 2 or heat it in a well-greased covered pan over a low heat. You can cut leftover leek tart into thin slices, bake in a preheated oven at 120°C/250°F/Gas $^{1}/_{2}$ until crisp and then add them to a light vegetable soup or a fresh salad.

Courgette patties with pepper cream

Exquisite

Serves 2
1 egg
1 egg yolk
45 ml/3 tablespoons single cream
60 ml/4 tablespoons dry white wine
*   or 60 ml/4 tablespoons water and*
*   5 ml/1 teaspoon lemon juice*
25 g/1 oz Parmesan cheese,
*   freshly grated*
115 g/4 oz plain wholemeal flour
1/2 bunch of dill
1 medium green pepper, seeded
*   and diced*
2 small ripe tomatoes, seeded
*   and diced*
1 bunch of fresh chives,
*   finely chopped*
200 ml/7 fl oz soured cream
2 garlic cloves
pinch of cayenne pepper
250 g/9 oz baby courgettes
2.5 ml/1/2 teaspoon chilli powder
30 ml/2 tablespoons sunflower oil
45 ml/3 tablespoons sesame seeds
herb salt
mixed salad leaves, to serve

Approximately per portion:
3,300 kj/790 kcal
28 g protein
51 g fat
51 g carbohydrate
13 g fibre

● Approximate preparation
time: 1 1/4 hours

1. Beat the whole egg with the egg yolk, cream, wine or water and lemon juice, cheese and flour in a large bowl to a thick, smooth batter. Cover and set aside for about 30 minutes.

2. For the pepper cream, set aside 1 dill sprig for the garnish and chop the remainder. Mix together the green pepper, tomatoes, chives, chopped dill and soured cream in a serving bowl. Crush 1 garlic clove and stir it in with the cayenne. Season to taste with salt. Garnish with the reserved dill sprig, cover with clear film and set aside in the refrigerator until ready to serve.

3. Finely grate the courgettes and stir them into the batter. Crush the remaining garlic and stir it into the batter with the chilli powder. Season to taste with salt. Transfer the batter to a jug.

4. Heat the oil in a large, heavy-based frying pan. Pour in about 30 ml/2 tablespoons of batter at a time and spread it into a flat patty. Sprinkle with sesame seeds and gently press them in. Fry the patties over a medium heat until golden brown on both sides. Remove them from the pan and keep warm while you cook the remaining patties in the same way.

5. Serve the patties hot, with the pepper cream, accompanied by mixed salad leaves.

Variation
Instead of courgettes, you can mix any other finely grated vegetable into the batter. Try carrots, leeks, celeriac or potatoes.

Tip

Peppers are very nutritious vegetables and contain even more vitamin C than fresh oranges. Red and orange peppers are also a valuable source of the antioxidant carotene – pro-vitamin A – which is thought to help protect against a number of diseases, including some cancers.

Courgette patties taste delicious and remain juicy after baking. Served with a cool cream sauce, they are an ideal summer dish.

Celery with crème fraîche

Easy

Serves 2
400 g/14 oz celery
10 ml/2 teaspoons butter
1 medium onion, chopped
1 garlic clove, finely chopped
30 ml/2 tablespoons water
7.5 ml/1¹/₂ teaspoons vegetable
    stock granules
45–60 ml/3–4 tablespoons
    crème fraîche
30 ml/2 tablespoons chopped
    fresh parsley
pinch of freshly grated nutmeg
sea salt
Onion and nut rice (see page 36),
    Green spelt grain patties (see
    page 34) or potatoes, to serve

Approximately per portion:
1,100 kj/260 kcal
6 g protein
21 g fat
11 g carbohydrate
6 g fibre

● Approximate preparation
   time: 35 minutes

1. Cut off and reserve the celery leaves. Cut any thick celery sticks in half lengthways, then chop all the sticks into 2 cm/³/₄ inch wide strips. Cut the celery leaves into strips and set aside.

2. Melt the butter in a heavy-based saucepan and fry the onion and garlic over a low heat, stirring occasionally, for 5 minutes. Add the chopped celery, water and the vegetable stock granules, cover and simmer over a medium heat for about 3 minutes.

3. Stir in the celery leaves and cook for a further 8–10 minutes, stirring once.

4. Remove the pan from the heat. Stir in the crème fraîche, parsley and nutmeg and season to taste with salt. Serve immediately with onion and nut rice, green spelt grain patties or potatoes.

Kohlrabi stew with curried oats

Easy

Kohlrabi is a root vegetable and a member of the extensive cabbage family. It is extremely popular in Germany and eastern Europe, but not very highly prized in Britain. Look for young, small specimens which have a pleasant nutty flavour with a slight hint of both cabbage and turnip. In fact, kohlrabi's alternative name is turnip cabbage.

Serves 2
150 g/5 oz oats
250 ml/8 fl oz water
10 ml/2 teaspoons vegetable
    stock granules
3.75 ml/³/₄ teaspoon curry powder
130 g/4¹/₂ oz spring onions
15 g/¹/₂ oz butter
400 g/14 oz kohlrabi, cut into
    1 cm/¹/₂ inch thick slices
22.5 ml/3¹/₂ teaspoons coarsely
    chopped hazelnuts
22.5 ml/3¹/₂ teaspoons
    sunflower seeds
105 ml/7 tablespoons single cream
1 tablespoon chopped fresh parsley
sea salt

Approximately per portion:
2,700 kj/640 kcal
19 g protein
36 g fat
60 g carbohydrate
10 g fibre

● Approximate preparation
   time: 40 minutes, plus soaking

1. Rinse the oats under cold running water, turn them into a saucepan, add the water and set aside to soak for 6–10 hours or overnight. Bring the oats to the boil and simmer over a low heat for about 10 minutes. Stir in 5 ml/1 teaspoon of the stock granules and the curry powder and set aside for 10–15 minutes.

2. Cut off and reserve the top one-third of the spring onions and slice the remainder diagonally into 1 cm/¹/₂ inch slices.

3. Melt the butter in a pan and add 60 ml/4 tablespoons water and the remaining stock granules. Add the sliced spring onions and the kohlrabi, cover and simmer over a medium heat for about 10 minutes. until the vegetables are tender, but still firm to bite.

4. Meanwhile, dry-fry the nuts and sunflower seeds in a heavy-based frying pan over a medium heat, stirring frequently, until golden.

5. Mix the oats, nut mixture, cream and parsley with the vegetables. Season with salt. Slice the reserved spring onions and sprinkle them on top.

Above: Celery with crème fraîche
Below: Kohlrabi stew with curried oats

Fried aubergines with chick-peas

Exquisite • Rather time-consuming

Serves 2
150 g/5 oz chick-peas
1 bay leaf
350 ml/12 fl oz water
75 ml/5 tablespoons extra virgin
   olive oil
150 g/5 oz onions, halved and
   thinly sliced
2 garlic cloves, finely chopped
2.5 ml/1/2 teaspoon ground turmeric
pinch of crushed pink peppercorns
pinch of ground cardamom
2.5 ml/1/2 teaspoon ground cumin
pinch of cayenne pepper
200 g/7 oz aubergines, cut into
   1 cm/1/2 inch slices
7.5 ml/11/2 teaspoons dried oregano
300 g/11 oz ripe tomatoes, sliced
10 ml/2 teaspoons fresh
thyme leaves
salt and freshly ground black pepper

Approximately per portion:
2,200 kj/520 kcal
19 g protein
28 g fat
50 g carbohydrate
14 g fibre

● Approximate preparation
   time: 1 1/4 hours, plus soaking

Tip

When buying aubergines, look
for specimens with an
unblemished, glossy skin and
which feel firm to the touch.
Store them in the refrigerator.

1. Put the chick-peas with the bay leaf in a large saucepan, pour in the water and set aside to soak overnight. Add a pinch of salt, bring to the boil, cover and simmer over a low heat for 40–50 minutes. Drain the chick-peas, reserving the cooking liquid. Remove and discard the bay leaf.

2. Heat 30 ml/2 tablespoons of the oil in a frying pan and fry the onion and garlic over a low heat, stirring occasionally, for 5 minutes. Stir in the turmeric, crushed pepper, cardamom, cumin and cayenne. Stir the onion mixture into the chick-peas and season to taste with salt.

3. Heat 30 ml/2 tablespoons of the remaining oil in a large frying pan. Turn the aubergine slices in the oil to coat and place them side by side in a single layer. Season with salt and pepper and sprinkle on half the oregano.

4. Spread the chick-peas on top of the aubergines and add 30 ml/2 tablespoons of the reserved cooking liquid. Cover and simmer for about 5 minutes. Place the tomato slices on top of the chick peas and season with salt. Scatter over the remaining oregano and the thyme, drizzle with the remaining oil and simmer for a further 5 minutes.

Courgette and potato soufflé

Easy

This soufflé works best with large courgettes, which are less watery than the small ones. If you prepare the dish in a flameproof casserole, you will not need to transfer it to a serving dish.

Serves 2
22.5 ml/3¹/2 teaspoons sunflower
    oil
115 g/4 oz onions, chopped
2 garlic cloves, finely chopped
350 g/12 oz courgettes
10 g/¹/4 oz butter
300 g/11 oz floury potatoes
50 g/2 oz Gouda cheese
50 g/2 oz Tilsit cheese
45 ml/3 tablespoons coarsely
    chopped mixed fresh herbs, such
    as parsley, lovage, basil, marjoram
    or oregano and thyme
2.5 ml/¹/2 teaspoon paprika
90 ml/6 tablespoons single cream
1 egg
30 ml/2 tablespoons freshly grated
    Parmesan cheese
30 ml/2 tablespoons toasted
    sunflower seeds
sea salt and freshly ground
    black pepper
Savoy cabbage with fennel and
    tomatoes (see page 10),
    to serve

Approximately per portion:
3,000 kj/710 kcal
30 g protein
51 g fat
35 g carbohydrate
8 g fibre

● Approximate preparation
   time: 1 hour

1. Heat the sunflower oil in a large, flameproof casserole. Add the onions and half the garlic and fry over a low heat, stirring occasionally, for 5 minutes. Peel the courgettes, if necessary, cut them in half lengthways and scoop out the soft insides.

2. Add the butter to the onions and grate the potatoes and courgettes into the casserole. Preheat the oven to 200°C/400°F/ Gas 6.

3. Put the Gouda, Tilsit and herbs into a food processor and process briefly. Stir the cheese mixture into the casserole. Stir in the paprika and season to taste with salt and pepper. Remove the casserole from the heat.

4. Beat the cream with the egg, the remaining garlic and a pinch of salt. Pour the mixture into the casserole and sprinkle the Parmesan and the sunflower seeds on top. Bake for about 30 minutes until golden brown. Serve immediately with Savoy cabbage with fennel and tomatoes.

Leeks with hazelnuts

Quick

Serves 2
15 ml/1 tablespoon sunflower oil
60 ml/4 tablespoons water
500 g/1¼ lb leeks, halved
    lengthways and cut into
    2 cm/¾ inch wide strips
10 ml/2 teaspoons vegetable
    stock granules
20 g/¾ oz butter
75 g/3 oz hazelnuts,
    roughly chopped
1.5–2.5 ml/¼–½ teaspoon
    chilli powder
2.5 ml/½ teaspoon dried marjoram
2 tablespoons chopped fresh parsley
Nutty cheese potatoes (see
    page 52), to serve

Approximately per portion:
1,700 kj/400 kcal
10 g protein
36 g fat
13 g carbohydrate
8 g fibre

● Approximate preparation
  time: 25 minutes

---

1. Heat the sunflower oil and water in a large saucepan. Add the leeks and the stock granules. Bring to the boil, cover and simmer over a medium heat for 8–10 minutes, until tender.

2. Meanwhile, melt the butter in a small, heavy-based frying pan and fry the nuts over a medium heat until golden. Stir the nuts, chilli powder and marjoram into the leeks. Sprinkle on the parsley. Serve immediately with nutty cheese potatoes.

Variation
These leeks are also very tasty if you omit the butter and nuts and stir in 60 ml/4 tablespoons crème fraîche instead.

Italian-style fennel

Easy

Serves 2
2 small fennel bulbs
30 ml/2 tablespoons virgin
    olive oil
1 green pepper, seeded and diced
60 ml/4 tablespoon vegetable stock
4 fresh rosemary needles, chopped
5 ml/1 teaspoon fresh thyme leaves
2.5 ml/½ teaspoon dried oregano
2 ripe, firm tomatoes
1 garlic clove, crushed
15 ml/1 tablespoon pine nuts
sea salt
brown rice, polenta, millet or
    potatoes, to serve

Approximately per portion:
890 kj/210 kcal
6 g protein
14 g fat
16 g carbohydrate
8 g fibre

● Approximate preparation
  time: 35 minutes

---

1. Cut off and reserve the feathery fronds for the garnish and cut the fennel bulbs into quarters.

2. Heat the oil in a saucepan. Add the fennel and green pepper and fry over a medium heat for about 5 minutes. Add the vegetable stock, rosemary, thyme and oregano and season to taste with salt. Cover and simmer over a low heat for 12–15 minutes.

3. Meanwhile, cut the tomatoes into eight wedges. Add them to the fennel mixture with the garlic, stir gently and simmer for a further 5 minutes.

4. Dry-fry the pine nuts in a heavy-based frying pan over a medium heat, stirring constantly.

5. Transfer the fennel mixture to a warm serving dish, sprinkle the pine nuts over the top and garnish with the reserved fennel fronds. Serve with brown rice, polenta, millet or potatoes.

Tip

Serve the fennel lukewarm as a starter or as part of a cold buffet with pitta bread.

Above: Leeks with hazelnuts
Below: Italian-style fennel

Pea pancakes with Caribbean topping

Exquisite • Rather time-consuming

Although related to bananas, plantains are larger, blander in flavour and contain more starch.

Serves 2
For the pancakes:
115 g/4 oz dried green peas
25 g/1 oz cornflour
2.5 ml/¹/2 teaspoon
  ground coriander
3.75 ml/³/4 teaspoon herb salt
3.75 ml/³/4 teaspoon curry powder
75 ml/5 tablespoons hot water
60 ml/4 tablespoons soured cream
20 ml/4 teaspoons sunflower oil

For the vegetables:
115 g/4 oz yellow peppers,
  halved and seeded
20 g/³/4 oz butter
115 g/4 oz onions, chopped
1–2 garlic cloves, finely chopped
1 fresh green chilli, seeded and
  finely chopped
115 g/4 oz ripe tomatoes, diced
2.5 ml/¹/2 teaspoon herb salt
2 medium plantains
1.5 ml/¹/4 teaspoon chilli powder
1.5 ml/¹/4 teaspoon
  ground cardamom
2.5 ml/¹/2 teaspoon paprika
2.5 ml/¹/2 teaspoon curry powder
7.5 ml/1¹/2 teaspoons grated
  lemon rind
15 ml/1 tablespoon lemon juice
15 ml/1 tablespoon chopped fresh
  lemon balm
15–30 ml/1–2 tablespoons
  sesame seeds
mixed leaf salad, to serve

Approximately per portion:
3,000 kj/710 kcal
20 g protein
1 g fat
75 g carbohydrate
12 g fibre

Sprouting time: 3 days

● Approximate preparation
   time: 1 hour, plus sprouting

1. Start sprouting the peas 3 days before you want to prepare the dish (see page 7).

2. Combine the cornflour, ground coriander, salt and curry powder in a bowl. Stir in the hot water and soured cream to form a smooth paste. Place the germinated peas in a food processor, process to a purée and mix with the cornflour paste. Set aside until required.

3. Cut the pepper halves into 1 cm/¹/2 inch squares. Melt the butter in a large frying pan. Add the onions and garlic and fry over a low heat, stirring occasionally, for 5 minutes. Add the peppers, chilli and tomatoes and season with the salt. Cover and simmer over a low heat for about 5 minutes, until the vegetables are tender, but still firm to the bite.

4. Peel and slice the plantains, stir them into the pan and simmer for a further 1–2 minutes. Stir in the chilli powder, cardamom, paprika, curry powder, lemon rind, lemon juice and lemon balm.

5. Heat a little sunflower oil in a large, heavy-based frying pan. Add the pea mixture, 15–30 ml/1–2 tablespoons at a time, spread it out into a flat patty and sprinkle with sesame seeds. Cover and fry the little pancakes over a low heat for about 5 minutes, until the undersides are golden brown. Turn them over, using a fish slice, add a little more oil, if necessary and finish frying them uncovered.

6. Serve the pancakes immediately with the vegetable topping and a mixed leaf salad.

Tip

Plantains are also known as cooking bananas and are available from Caribbean markets and specialist supermarkets. They vary in colour from green, through yellow to black. Green bananas may be used as a substitute.

Both components of this dish sound exotic: pancakes made from a corn batter with sprouting peas and a topping of onions, plantains, peppers and tomatoes. Tastes wonderful!

Green peppers with carrots

Easy

Serves 2
30 ml/2 tablespoons sunflower oil
115 g/4 oz onions, chopped
150 g/5 oz carrots, cut into
    thin strips
300 g/11 oz green peppers, seeded
    and cut into thin strips
7.5 ml/1 1/2 teaspoons vegetable
    stock granules
5 ml/1 teaspoon fresh thyme leaves
60 ml/4 tablespoons water
2.5 ml/1/2 teaspoon dried oregano
15 ml/1 tablespoon chopped
    fresh parsley
30–45 ml/2–3 tablespoons
    crème fraîche
herb salt
brown rice or millet, Pea pancakes
    with Caribbean topping
    (see page 48) or Spicy corn
    soufflé (see page 34), to serve

Approximately per portion:
1,050 kj/250 kcal
4 g protein
20 g fat
18 g carbohydrate
7 g fibre

● Approximate preparation
  time: 35 minutes

---

1. Heat the sunflower oil in a large, heavy-based saucepan. Add the onions and fry over a low heat, stirring occasionally, for 5 minutes.

2. Add the carrots, green peppers, stock granules, thyme and water. Cover and simmer over a low heat for 12–15 minutes, until the vegetables are tender, but still firm to the bite.

3. Stir in the oregano and parsley and season to taste with salt. Stir in the crème fraîche and heat gently for 1–2 minutes.

4. Serve immediately with plain brown rice or millet, pea pancakes with Caribbean topping or spicy corn soufflé.

Spicy Savoy cabbage

Easy

Serves 2
400 g/14 oz Savoy cabbage
25 g/1 oz butter
50 g/2 oz onion, chopped
1.5 ml/1/4 teaspoon coriander
    seeds, lightly crushed
1.5 ml/1/4 teaspoon chilli powder
60 ml/4 tablespoons water
7.5 ml/1 1/2 teaspoons vegetable
    stock granules
10 ml/2 teaspoons fresh
    thyme leaves
2 chopped fresh lovage leaves
15 ml/1 tablespoon chopped
    fresh parsley
sea salt
Nutty cheese potatoes (see
    page 52) or mashed potatoes,
    to serve

Approximately per portion:
760 kj/180 kcal
6 g protein
13 g fat
10 g carbohydrate
8 g fibre

● Approximate preparation
  time: 40 minutes

---

1. Cut out the cabbage stalk and grate the tender part. Cut the cabbage leaves into 2 cm/3/4 inch wide strips.

2. Melt 10 g/1/4 oz of the butter in a saucepan and fry the onion over a low heat, stirring occasionally, for 5 minutes. Crush the coriander seeds in the mortar with a pestle or with a rolling pin. Stir the crushed coriander seeds and chilli powder into the onion and add the cabbage. Fry, stirring frequently, for a further 1–2 minutes.

3. Add the water, stock granules, thyme and lovage, cover and simmer over a low heat for about 15 minutes, until the vegetables are tender, but still firm to the bite. Stir once during cooking.

4. Add the remaining butter to the vegetables, taste and add a little salt, if necessary, and sprinkle with parsley. Serve with nutty cheese potatoes or mashed potatoes.

Above: Green peppers with carrots
Below: Spicy Savoy cabbage

Potato salad with green beans

Rather time-consuming

This delicious salad tastes best served lukewarm with plenty of fresh thyme.

Serves 2
300 g/11 oz small, waxy
*   potatoes, unpeeled*
200 g/7 oz young green beans
120 ml/4 fl oz water
7.5 ml/1 1/2 teaspoons vegetable
*   stock granules*
8 fresh thyme sprigs
5 ml/1 teaspoon Dijon mustard
45 ml/3 tablespoons cider vinegar
30 ml/2 tablespoons sunflower oil
10 ml/2 teaspoons fresh
*   thyme leaves*
1 small onion, finely chopped
15 ml/1 tablespoon chopped
*   mixed fresh parsley, tarragon*
*   and marjoram*
10 ml/2 teaspoons butter
2 eggs
sea salt and freshly ground
*   black pepper*

Approximately per portion:
1,500 kj/360 kcal
12 g protein
19 g fat
32 g carbohydrate
7 g fibre

● Approximate preparation
   time: 1 1/4 hours

---

1. Put the potatoes in a saucepan and add just enough water to cover. Bring to the boil, cover and simmer over a medium heat for 15–20 minutes, until just tender.

Drain well and set aside to cool slightly. When cool enough to handle, peel and slice them.

2. Meanwhile, trim the beans and cut them into 2.5 cm/1 inch long pieces. Place them in a saucepan and add the water, stock granules and thyme sprigs. Bring to the boil, then simmer for 10–15 minutes, until the beans are tender, but still firm to bite. Drain the beans, reserving the cooking liquid.

3. Place the sliced potatoes and beans in a large dish. Mix 45 ml/3 tablespoons of the reserved cooking liquid with the mustard, vinegar, oil, thyme leaves and onion. Pour this dressing over the potatoes and beans, season to taste with salt and pepper and toss lightly to coat.

4. Cover and set the salad aside for about 30 minutes. Add the mixed herbs.

5. Melt the butter in a frying pan and lightly fry the eggs. Divide the salad between two serving plates, top with an egg and serve.

Nutty cheese potatoes

Easy

Served with a selection of fresh vegetables, this substantial dish is a meal in itself.

Serves 2
500 g/1 1/4 lb waxy
*   potatoes, unpeeled*
20 g/3/4 oz butter
75 g/3 oz hazelnuts or walnuts,
*   roughly chopped*
75 g/3 oz Gruyère cheese, grated
salt and freshly ground black pepper
spices to taste, such as ground
*   fenugreek or chilli powder or*
*   roughly chopped fresh herbs to*
*   taste, such as marjoram, thyme*
*   or sage*

Approximately per portion:
2,650 kj/630 kcal
21 g protein
41 g fat
45 g carbohydrate
9 g fibre

● Approximate preparation
   time: 40 minutes

---

1. Put the potatoes in a saucepan and add just enough water to cover. Bring to the boil, cover and simmer over a medium heat for about 15 minutes, until they are just tender. Drain well and set aside to cool slightly. When cool enough to handle, peel them.

2. Melt the butter in a large frying pan. Grate the potatoes into it, add a pinch of salt and gently stir in the nuts. Fry over a medium heat, stirring gently once or twice, for about 10 minutes.

3. Stir in the cheese and season to taste with salt and pepper and with spices or fresh herbs to taste. Serve immediately.

Above: Nutty cheese potatoes
Below: Potato salad with green beans

Delicatessen potatoes

The first new potatoes, boiled in their skins and served with fresh butter and herbs or with a spicy creamy cheese, are really delicious. To serve 2, boil 500 g/1 1/4 lb new potatoes and serve them with one of the following accompaniments and a large bowl of mixed salad leaves. This is a full meal with an ideal protein combination.

Preparation is the same for all the recipes. Stir the curd cheese with the cream or the sunflower oil and milk to make a creamy dressing. Then gradually add the other ingredients. Finally, season with the spices and garnish.

The nutritional information in each recipe is given for the dressing only and does not include the potatoes.

Blue-veined cheese cream

Exquisite

Serves 2
200 g/7 oz curd cheese
75 g/3 oz single cream
200 g/7 oz Roquefort or Danish
*   Blue cheese, mashed*
*   with a fork*
4 walnuts, to garnish

Approximately per portion:
2,600 kj/620 kcal
38 g protein
48 g fat
6 g carbohydrate
1 g fibre
● Approximate preparation time: 10 minutes

Herb cheese

Quick

Serves 2
250 g/9 oz curd cheese
105 ml/7 tablespoons soured cream
5 ml/1 teaspoon yeast extract
1 garlic clove, crushed
1 gherkin, finely diced
45 ml/3 tablespoons chopped fresh
*   mixed herbs, such as parsley or*
*   chervil, chives, lemon balm, dill,*
*   borage, lovage and basil*
2.5 ml/1/2 teaspoon
*   ground fenugreek*
radish slices or lamb's lettuce,
*   to garnish*

Approximately per portion:
710 kj/170 kcal
20 g protein
6 g fat
10 g carbohydrate
1 g fibre
● Approximate preparation time: 15 minutes

Celery cheese

Easy

250 g/9 oz curd cheese
30 ml/2 tablespoons milk
30 ml/2 tablespoons sunflower oil
115 g/4 oz celery, finely chopped
30 ml/2 tablespoons chopped
*   fresh parsley*
15 ml/1 tablespoon Dijon
*   mustard*
2.5 ml/1/2 teaspoon yeast extract
15 ml/1 tablespoon lemon juice
sea salt

Approximately per portion:
1,000 kj/240 kcal
17 g protein
15 g fat
10 g carbohydrate
1 g fibre
● Approximate preparation time: 15 minutes

Pepper cheese

Easy

Serves 2
250 g/9 oz curd cheese
75 ml/5 tablespoons single cream
15 ml/1 tablespoon finely
*   chopped onion*
50 g/2 oz red pepper, seeded and
*   finely chopped*
50 g/2 oz green pepper, seeded and
*   finely chopped*
1 large gherkin, finely chopped
2.5 ml/1/2 teaspoon Dijon mustard
1 garlic clove, crushed
5 ml/1 teaspoon chilli powder
2.5 ml/1/2 teaspoon paprika
3.75 ml/3/4 teaspoon herb salt

Approximately per portion:
760 kj/180 kcal
18 g protein
7 g fat
10 g carbohydrate
1 g fibre
● Approximate preparation time: 15 minutes

Top: Pepper cheese
Second: Celery cheese
Third: Herb cheese
Bottom: Blue-veined cheese cream

Rhubarb crumble

Rather time-consuming

Serves 3–4
50 g/2 oz blanched almonds,
roughly chopped
185 g/6¹/2 oz plain
wholemeal flour
1.5 ml/¹/4 teaspoon
ground cinnamon
75 g/3 oz chilled butter, diced
115–130 g/4–4¹/2 oz clear honey
sunflower oil, for brushing
300 g/11 oz rhubarb
250 g/9 oz apples
1 egg white

Approximately per portion:
2,910 kj 695 kcal
13 g protein
34 g fat
51 g carbohydrate
11 g fibre

● Approximate preparation
time: 1 hour 20 minutes

1. Put the almonds into a large bowl and sift in the flour and cinnamon. Tip in any bran remaining in the sieve and mix well. Add the butter and rub it into the mixture with your fingertips. Gradually stir in 75–90g/3–3¹/2 oz of the honey and knead well until combined into a crumbly texture. It is easier to do this using an electric mixer fitted with a dough hook than by hand.

2. Place the crumble in a metal bowl, cover and place in the freezer until the fruit is ready.

3. Brush a 25 cm/10 inch round pie dish with oil. Cut any thick rhubarb stalks in half lengthways, then cut all the stalks into 1–2 cm/ ¹/2–³/4 inch pieces. Place them in the prepared dish.

4. Quarter and core the apples and then coarsely grate them. Stir the apples into the rhubarb. Drizzle 15 ml/1 tablespoon of the remaining honey over the fruit, then spoon the crumble on top, pressing it down gently with the back of the spoon.

5. Cover the dish with foil and put it into a cold oven. Bake the crumble at 180°C/350°F/Gas 4 for about 25 minutes. Remove the foil and bake the crumble for a further 10 minutes.

6. Meanwhile, whisk the egg white until stiff. Gradually drizzle in 7.5 ml/1¹/2 teaspoons of the remaining honey, whisking constantly until stiff and glossy. Spoon the meringue into a piping bag and decorate the top of the crumble with it.

7. Return the crumble to the oven and bake for a further 5–10 minutes until the meringue topping is golden brown. Serve the rhubarb crumble warm.

Blackcurrant and banana cream

Quick

Serves 2
75 ml/5 tablespoons double cream
1 large banana
45 ml/3 tablespoons natural yogurt
45 ml/3 tablespoons unsweetened
blackcurrant juice
5 ml/1 teaspoon clear honey,
preferably acacia blossom
1.5 ml/¹/4 teaspoon grated
orange rind
1 large eating apple
15 ml/1 tablespoon chopped
unsalted pistachio nuts,
to decorate

Approximately per portion:
1,300 kj/310 kcal
5 g protein
17 g fat
36 g carbohydrate
3 g fibre

● Approximate preparation
time: 15 minutes

1. Beat the cream until stiff. Peel and roughly chop the banana and place it in a food processor with the yogurt, blackcurrant juice, honey and orange rind. Process to a purée, then scrape into a serving bowl. Fold in the cream.

2. Quarter and core the apple and slice thinly. Fold the apple slices into the cream mixture. Sprinkle the pistachio nuts on top.

Above: Rhubarb crumble
Below: Blackcurrant and banana cream

Cornmeal cream with mixed berries

Easy

Serves 4–6
150 g/5 oz coarse cornmeal
475 ml/16 fl oz water
2.5 ml/1/2 teaspoon vanilla essence
200 ml/7 fl oz milk
45 ml/3 tablespoons clear honey
50 g/2 oz hazelnuts or almonds,
*   coarsely ground*
grated rind of 1 lemon
500 g/1 1/4 lb mixed berries,
*   such as strawberries, raspberries ,*
*   loganberries and blackberries*
75 ml/5 tablespoons double cream

Approximately per portion:
1,070 kj/255 kcal
6 g protein 11 g fat
34 g carbohydrate
3 g fibre

● Approximate preparation
   time: 40 minutes

1. Mix the cornmeal with the water and vanilla essence in a saucepan. Bring to the boil, over a medium heat, stirring constantly, and cook for about 2 minutes. Turn off the heat, but leave the pan on the hob for 10–15 minutes.

2. Stir the milk into the pan with 30 ml/2 tablespoons of the honey, the ground hazelnuts or almonds and the lemon rind. Set aside to cool completely.

3. Prepare the fruit and, if necessary, drizzle it with a little of the remaining honey to sweeten. Beat the cream until stiff and fold it

into the cold cornmeal mixture. Serve the cornmeal cream with the mixed berries.

Apple pancakes with pear spread

Rather time-consuming

Serves 2
115 g/4 oz spelt flour or
*   wholemeal flour*
120 ml/4 fl oz milk
30 ml/2 tablespoons currants
5 ml/1 teaspoon clear honey
10 ml/2 teaspoons melted butter
2 small eggs, separated
2.5 ml/1/2 teaspoon
*   ground cinnamon*
5 ml/1 teaspoon finely grated
*   lemon rind*
200 g/7 oz eating apples
sunflower oil, for frying
30 ml/2 tablespoons desiccated or
*   grated fresh coconut*
30–45 ml/2–3 tablespoons
*   pear spread*

Approximately per portion:
2,600 kj/620 kcal
16 g protein
31 g fat
69 g carbohydrate
8 g fibre

● Approximate preparation
   time: 1 hour 10 minutes

1. Sift the flour into a bowl and tip in any bran remaining in the sieve. Add the milk, currants, honey, butter, egg yolks, ground cinnamon and grated lemon rind. Stir thoroughly to mix and set aside for about 30 minutes.

2. Beat the egg whites until stiff peaks form, then fold them into the batter in the bowl. Quarter and core the apples, then cut them into thin slices.

3. Heat a little sunflower oil in a small frying pan. Arrange a quarter of the apple slices in a single layer, then cover with about 30 ml/ 2 tablespoons of the batter and sprinkle with a quarter of the coconut. Cover and fry over a low heat, until golden brown on the underside and the pancake comes away easily from the base of the frying pan.

4. Turn the pancake over with a fish slice, add a little more oil to the frying pan and fry the pancake until the other side is golden brown. Slide out on to a serving plate and cook 3 more pancakes in the same way. Top the pancakes with pear spread and serve.

Tip

If you want to make pancakes without the apple, add 60 ml/ 4 tablespoons milk to the batter.

Below: Cornmeal cream with
mixed berries
Above: Apple pancakes with pear spread

Hazel and almond cake

For guests • Easy

This is a particularly fine cake recipe with many possible variations. If wrapped in foil, before decoration, it will keep in the refrigerator for about 2 weeks.

Makes 1 x 30 cm/12 inch long cake
100 g/3³/4 oz butter, melted
150g/5 oz brown sugar
6 eggs, separated
1.5 ml/1¹/4 teaspoon
   ground cinnamon
grated rind of 1 lemon
105 ml/7 tablespoons milk
30 ml/2 tablespoons rum
250 g/9 oz plain wholemeal flour
7.5 ml/1¹/2 teaspoons cream
   of tartar
sunflower oil, for brushing
115 g/4 oz hazelnuts, finely ground
130 g/4¹/2 oz blanched almonds,
   finely ground

Approximately per slice:
1,120 kj/270 kcal
7 g protein
16 g fat
21 g carbohydrate
3 g fibre

● Approximate preparation
   time: 1 hour 20 minutes

1. Beat the butter with the sugar, egg yolks, cinnamon and lemon rind until foamy. Add the milk and rum. Mix the flour with the cream of tartar, sift it into the mixture and stir well.

2. Preheat the oven to 180°C/350°F/Gas 4. Line a 30 cm/12 inch long cake tin with greaseproof paper and brush with oil. Combine the hazelnuts and almonds in a bowl. Beat the egg whites until stiff peaks form. Gradually fold the nuts and egg whites alternately into the cake mixture.

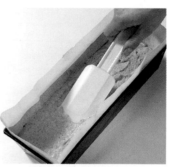

3. Spoon the mixture into the prepared tin and gently smooth the surface with a spatula.

4. Bake the cake for about 40 minutes, or until a fine skewer inserted into the centre of the cake comes out clean. Leave the cake to cool in the tin.

Variations

Strawberry-cream slices

Turn the cooled cake out of the tin and cut it into slices. Sprinkle each slice with orange liqueur or orange juice and add some strawberries, sweetened with honey. Decorate by piping with whipped cream and top with more strawberries. Sprinkle chopped unsalted pistachio nuts around the edges.

Petit fours

Spoon the cake mixture into little paper cake cases, instead of a tin, and sprinkle flaked almonds on top. Bake in a preheated oven at 180°C/350°F/Gas 4 for about 20 minutes.

Cherry cake

Halve the quantity, add 10 ml/ 2 teaspoons cocoa powder and omit the milk. Make the cake mixture and spoon it into a greased loose-based cake tin. Top with 500 g/1¼ lb stoned, drained canned cherries. Bake in a preheated oven at 180°C/350°F/ Gas 4 for 40–45 minutes. Decorate with whipped cream.

Damson or apple cake

Spoon the cake mixture on to a greased baking sheet and smooth the surface. Arrange stoned halved damsons or apple slices on top. Brush the fruit with clear honey. Bake in a preheated oven at 180°C/350°F/Gas 4 for about 40 minutes.

Tip

The cake freezes well, so it is worth making the full quantity of the mixture, even if you only use half for a particular recipe. If you do not want to use rum, you can use orange juice and a little grated orange rind instead.

Great Little Cook Books
Wholefood

Published originally under the title
Vollwertkost by Gräfe und Unzer
Verlag GmbH, München

©1991 by Gräfe und Unzer Verlag
GmbH, München

English-language edition
© 2001 by Transedition Limited,
Oxford, England

This edition published in 2001 by
Advanced Marketing,
Bicester, Oxfordshire

Translation:
Translate-A-Book, Oxford

Editing:
Linda Doeser Publishing Services,
London

Typesetting:
Organ Graphic, Abingdon

10 9 8 7 6 5 4 3 2 1
Printed in Dubai

ISBN 1 901683 18 4

Important note

If possible, buy only cleaned grain, containing no dirt or weed seeds, particularly not the poisonous corn cockle. Ergot, which has become increasingly prevalent, especially in rye, is clearly recognizable, blackish and usually a greatly enlarged seed. Consumed in large quantities, it can be life-threatening. It is extremely unlikely that any commercially available cereals and grains contain any dangerous substances.

Never eat raw pulses, apart from young peas. Phasin, the poison naturally present in pulses, is only rendered harmless by thorough cooking. In seedlings, this poison is only partly broken down, so sprouts grown from pulses should be briefly blanched and not consumed too often.

Note:
Quantities for all recipes are given in both metric and imperial measures and, if appropriate, in standard measuring spoons. They are not interchangeable, so readers should follow one set or the other.
5 ml = 1 teaspoon
15 ml = 1 tablespoon

Ingrid Früchtel

Since finishing her studies 20 years ago, Ingrid Früchtel has been working in the field of wholefoods, both in theory and practice. She passes on her wide experience conducting numerous courses and seminars. Through her successful books she has become a recognized authority on the subject. She lives in Oberfranken in a farmhouse with a large garden. Her daughter, Annette Früchtel, made a considerable contribution to this book.

Odette Teubner

was trained by her father, the internationally renowned food photographer Christian Teubner. Today, she works exclusively in the Teubner Studio for Food Photography. In her spare time she is an enthusiastic photographer of children, using her own son as her model.

Kerstin Mosny

trained in photography at a college in French-speaking Switzerland. She then worked as an assistant to various photographers, including the food photographer Jürgen Tapprich in Zürich. Since March 1985 she has worked in the Teubner Studio for Food Photography.